A Little Book of

Old Roses

Hazel Le Rougetel

Illustrated by

ROSEANNE SANDERS

Putnam

G.P. Putnam's Sons
Publishers Since 1838
200 Madison Avenue
New York, NY 10016

First American Edition 1992

Library of Congress Cataloging-in-Publication Data

Le Rougetel, Hazel
Little Book of Old Roses/Hazel Le Rougetel;
illustrated by Roseanne Sanders. — 1 American ed.
p.   cm.

ISBN 0-399-13787-4

Printed in the E.C.
1 2 3 4 5 6 7 8 9 10

Introduction

The last half of the twentieth century has witnessed a surge of interest in the older roses, largely due to stimulation by English rose grower Graham Thomas through his books and practical demonstration. For the National Trust he planned the extensive Rose Garden within mellowed walls at Mottisfont near Stockbridge in Hampshire, where rose history may be traced from his most beautiful presentation.

Heritage Rose Societies flourish in America, Australia and New Zealand; over four hundred enthusiasts attended an International Conference in Christchurch in 1990. The Royal National Rose Society has recently formed an Historic Roses Group to emphasise its concern for all classes, which are well represented in its Gardens of the Rose near St. Albans, Hertfordshire. In North America there is a comprehensive collection at the Morton Arboretum, Lisle, Illinois and another, very attractively displayed, can be seen in the Cranford Memorial Rose Garden, Brooklyn Botanic Garden, New York.

This little book aims to tell the story of rose development from medieval times to the beginning of this century, with emphasis on those varieties cherished by mankind. The twenty-eight old roses illustrated have been chosen as examples of the main classes and these are augmented by mention of one hundred more in the text – almost all available today. Guidance is given on how best to grow them informally as flowering shrubs of diverse form, and suggestions are made for suitable plants to use as complementary companions.

Rosa eglanteria

This European species has long been used in gardens, as shown at the Roman villa in Fishbourne, near Chichester, where it brightens surrounding evergreen planting. In medieval and Tudor times it embellished arbours and was one of the first roses to be taken abroad by colonists and often used as windbreak hedges in bleak country. William Penn's initial instructions to use "what grows quickest" included the sweet briar. President Jefferson planted many in his Virginian garden and landscaper "Capability" Brown included them for wilderness planting at Petworth, Sussex in the eighteenth century.

The sweet briar spans 12 x 8 ft and clear pink blooms are followed by shiny orange-red fruit; the fragrant fine foliage, its greatest asset, is intensified by rain and also by clipping. It will tolerate any condition, though perhaps looks best in grass or on woodland perimeter with *RR. canina*, *arvensis*, *villosa* and shorter *pimpinellifolia* to the fore – other European species and appropriate companions for Shakespeare's eglantine.

Early hybrids included two doubles of compact habit; Scarlet Sweet Briar is eye-catching with little scent, whereas pink-tinted Manning's Blush has more and a later introduction, Janet's Pride is semi-double with blush markings on bright pink flowers. A century ago, Lord Penzance bred a number of large, lax varieties only suitable for bigger gardens, one of the most attractive being Lady Penzance, tinted yellow, salmon, and copper.

The Apothecary's Rose

Long before "roses red and white" were recorded in early descriptions of gardens, this Gallica had been appreciated for its usefulness. By the thirteenth century it was grown extensively around Provins, near Paris, its scent-retaining petals used for a famed conserve and medicaments – *officinalis* denotes a plant approved by the apothecaries. In 1652, the English herbalist, Nicholas Culpeper, prescribed a "decoction of Red Roses" for pains in the head, eyes, throat, gums, head, and stomach, while John Winthrop, first governor of Massachusetts, advised his family, about to join him from England, to bring the conserve with them, and a friend sent roses pink, red, and white, to grow in his Boston garden.

Gallicas are the tidiest of old summer-flowering roses and suitable for small gardens with compact bushes, having rather rigid, rough-textured dark-green leaves and bristly stems. Wonderfully fragrant flowers – always poised on stiff stalks and ranging from palest blush through every shade of pink to deep maroon – they provide a galaxy of beauty over six weeks at midsummer.

The Apothecary's Rose was correctly grown with other herbs and the same association can be maintained today; small blue flowers of some herbs complement the deep tones of Gallicas. Hyssop, sage or rue can be planted with darkest Tuscany (also known as old velvet) and deep magenta conditorum, backed by rosemary with purple Cardinal de Richelieu and blush Duchesse de Montebello.

Rosa Mundi

In 1846 a leading American rose grower, William Prince of Flushing, New York listed 93 "striped, variegated, mottle or marbled" Gallicas. Comparatively few endured, unlike the earliest: Rosa Mundi. No agreement has been reached on how this name arose or on its first appearance, but Sir Thomas Hanmer stated, "first found in Norfolke a few years since, upon a branch of the common Red Rose and from thence multiplied" (*The Garden Book*, 1659). Like the Apothecary's Rose in every respect, except that the light crimson petals are striped with blush, this lovely rose has maintained a place in gardens ever since.

However, the majority of variegated Gallicas are double, their closely-packed petals arranged differently. Petals, for example, have defined deep-crimson markings in Tricolor de Flandre and rolling pale lilac towards a crimson center for Président de Sèze. Camaieux has a rather looser assembly, incurling with crimson and purple, and fading to magenta and lilac; an abundance of petals in Charles de Mills, seemingly shorn flat, are flushed with every deep, sumptuous shade.

A careful choice of companion is necessary for these charmers: a short flowering time warrants no distraction. Back them with shrubs of sober foliage – a viburnum or hardy hebe to flower before or after the roses – and underplant with discreet *Ajuga repens*, *Viola labradorica* or *Geranium sanguineum striatum*.

Céleste

If space dictated choice of one old summer-flowering rose to represent Albas (the tallest group, once known as "tree roses"), Céleste could well display their particular qualities. Making a good bush of some 6 x 4 ft with new, green wood, few prickles and beautiful soft grey-green foliage, they provide perfect foil for delicate pink blooms of pure fragrance. Semi-double, they unfurl gracefully from a perfectly scrolled bud to become slightly deeper in the center around a small group of golden stamens. Céleste, like all Albas, is comparatively disease free and tolerates harsh conditions.

The earliest of the group, *R. a. semi-plena*, the old white rose grown with the red Apothecary's in medieval times was taken by the House of York as its emblem, as was the other by the Lancastrians. It was also used in medicine, particularly for treating eyes, and in the perfume industry. *R.a. maxima*, known as Great Double White and also the Jacobite Rose on account of association with Bonnie Prince Charlie, has many petals of full blooms in darker glaucous foliage. The aptly named Great Maiden's Blush, with reflexing petals paling at the perimeter and of beguiling scent, has been a firm favorite over many years. Old Albas are well displayed as stalwart shrubs in a broad border at Castle Howard, near York, where phlox of soft shades infil after midsummer and glaucous hosta foliage blends below.

Königin von Dänemarck

New Albas were developed in the early nineteenth century, mostly fully double and of great charm, Queen of Denmark perhaps proving to be the best seducer. Victorian rosarian Thomas Rivers records "so much was this esteemed when first raised from seed that plants from Germany cost five guineas each in England". Deep pink on opening, reflexed blooms become softer around a button eye and are well displayed against dark glaucous foliage. An indisputable recommendation must be its choice by Graham Thomas for his midsummer buttonhole.

Twenty-one Albas were listed in the 1845 catalog of Hovery's Cambridge Nurseries, Boston, and include "superb Queen of Denmark" and "exquisite Félicité Parmentier". Of the two, the latter makes a slightly-smaller bush with unusual features: foliage is light green and buds have a yellow tint. This is lost when it opens to pale pink petals deepening inwards and fading to cream at the edges of a somewhat globular bloom. Madame Legras de St. Germain, more vigorous, is pristine white with unique yellow shading in the center of a very full flower. Later on, a smaller Alba, Pompon Blanc Parfait was introduced. With dainty pale-pink flowers fading to almost white and typical Alba foliage of appropriate scale on a 4 ft bush, this is well suited to limited space.

With all these roses, simple flowers such as campanula, foxglove, aquilegia, saponaria, and dianthus complete a satisfying picture.

Kazanlik

Accounts of sweetly-scented Damask roses date back to long ago in countries of the Eastern Mediterranean, although no English records appear until the sixteenth century, and they were probably taken to western America by early Spanish missionaries. A natural variation, or sport, from *R. damascena*, York and Lancaster, with irregular pink-and-white blotches, was believed to signify union of the two royal houses. Kazanlik, a summer-flowerer, gets its name from a district in Bulgaria, also known as the Valley of the Roses, stretching some sixty miles, where this rose has been grown extensively since the beginning of the eighteenth century for the attar of roses industry.

Quatre Saisons, or Autumn Damask (*R. damascena semperflorens*), is unique among old garden roses in flowering from June to October, and even earlier blooms of so-called "monthly roses" were forced against heated walls at Chelsea Physic Garden in the eighteenth century.

These early Damasks have loose, semi-double flowers, white or light pink (called *R. pallida* by the apothecaries) and slender hips compared with rotund and oval of Gallicas and Albas. Their foliage also differs. Round, soft, pale-green leaves on bristly stems form somewhat spindly, lax bushes, less desirable as garden roses than later hybrids. They are best grown naturally in a wild setting, placed behind a shrub on which they may tumble near a seat or path, where their alluring scent may be savored.

Madame Hardy

As with the Albas, there was a spate of new Damasks at the beginning of the nineteenth century. One raised from seed by the Superintendent of the Luxembourg Gardens, Paris, in 1832, was named Madame Hardy for his wife. At the time, Thomas Rivers of the Sawbridgeworth Nursery thought a more magnificent rose did not exist. Early praise also came from America and Canada for the full-petalled white roses with a green eye. Twentieth-century writers continue to commend it ecstatically. The large bush of 5 x 5 ft is lax and sometimes needs support.

Isapahan, slightly smaller, produces clear pink blooms in clusters on an upright bush, although Marie Louise, of the same size, is inclined to hang unusual purplish-pink heavy-headed flowers. This lovely Damask was produced at Malmaison, the Empress Josephine's famous rose garden. Leda, or Painted Damask, so called because carmine buds tip the white petals of a rounded flower, is unusually compact (3 x 3 ft and William Prince forecast in 1846 that it would be a favorite for some time. It is well shown, tidily bordering a lawn, at Mottisfont today.

These summer-flowering Damasks of various habit are well suited to mixed-border planting. To make the most of their flowering time, do not plant any distracting "hot" colors near their paler shades. One, perhaps Marie Louise, could be grown against a wall near a window or patio for maximum enjoyment of midsummer scent.

Rosa x centifolia

This historic rose had long been recorded before it was developed further in Holland during the seventeenth century, when it often appeared in Flemish flower paintings – one of its names is Rose des Peintres. In England, Centifolias have long been cherished. They were the best-selling roses of nurseries in the mid-eighteenth century, and fashionable Regency ladies liked to adorn their hair with a "full blown Provence Rose" (not to be confused with Provins, relating to Gallicas). William Paul, eminent Victorian rosarian, considered this class to produce some of the finest globular-shaped roses grown. The somewhat unflattering name of cabbage roses came about on account of their petals overlapping in that form when half open.

Two early nineteenth-century variations have unique characteristics. *R. c. bullata*, with extraordinary puckered foliage, bronze when young, is known as the lettuce-leaved rose, while *R. c. cristata* has the popular name of Chapeau de Napoléon, on account of the tricorne-shaped winged calyx. The lovely late flowerer, Unique Blanche, discovered in Suffolk in 1757, has almost transparent petals of fine, silky texture, and is mentioned in accounts of early colonial gardens.

Coarse, limp foliage and stout, well-armed stems make Centifolia bushes somewhat ungainly, but charm is maintained by strongly-fragrant, voluptuous flowers inclining their heads appealingly to billowing plants such as *Alchemilla mollis* in order to hide the lower supports.

Rose de Meaux

Some neater Centifolias are useful for growing in containers or for fronting a border, the smallest being clear pink de Meaux which has miniature flowers and foliage (2 x 2 ft). It was known before most of the hybrid Centifolias and also blooms earlier than they do (Rivers judged it "desirable for its spring-gladdening flowers"). Ombrée Parfait is slightly larger and provides a good contrast with its purple tones, its lax form fitting a wide tub. Petite d'Hollande may reach 4 ft but has excellent discipline, holding small, typical Centifolia-pink flowers erect in groups, which last well on a compact bush, thus making it suitable for a large terracotta pot. This trio will provide flowers for more than two months, provided four points are borne in mind: the container must be of adequate depth, drainage efficient, and the planting medium should be "open". Roses hate to have compacted roots, as happen with frequent watering – and this is the fourth essential proviso, especially necessary in hot climates. A good planting mixture consists of $1/2$ potting compost, $1/4$ each of fibre and grit, plus a handful of charcoal (remains of a wood fire or bonfire are useful) to replace the top 2–3 ins in spring.

Any of the smaller old roses, provided they are neat growers, are suitable for pots on a tiny garden patio where their scent may be enjoyed. When flowering is over, they can be replaced with container-grown plants of, for example, tender late-flowering fuchsias.

Common Moss

This rose first occurred as a Centifolia sport in Europe before the end of the seventeenth century. Philip Miller brought one back to Chelsea Physic Garden from Leiden in 1727 to wide acclaim, and mosses remained in demand when most old roses fell from favor during Victorian times. Robert Buist exhibited 20 varieties at the Pennsylvania Horticultural Society Show in June 1855. However, the Common Moss has always held its own, with fragrant pink flowers offset by soft, green-mossed flower stalks and buds, a unique feature due to enlarged glands, scented and sticky, varying from dark reddish brown to pale lime green in subsequent introductions.

These vary in color and size from the tiny, light crimson Little Gem and creamy pink Mouselline, both 3 ft, to lofty William Lobb, 8 ft or more if supported, which displays purple-lavender blooms to advantage. In between, Henri Martin presents deep crimson flowers in abundance on an open 6 ft, while Nuits de Young is shorter, with slender form, small maroon flowers and bronze-tinted foliage.

Mosses, and indeed all the old roses, should not be pruned hard like modern varieties. Aim to maintain well-formed shrubs by removing all spindly growth and cutting out old wood from the base at the end of July to encourage new, long shoots. These may be shortened by $1/3$ in February to present a balanced bush. However, Gallicas and Albas need less attention in this respect.

Double White (Scots Briar)

A small, hardy species, *R. pimpinellifolia*, flourishing on windswept shore or limestone heath, was used by two brothers to develop many varieties at a nursery near Perth in the early nineteenth century. Over 200 varieties were offered originally but, with the advent of long-flowering roses, their popularity declined, and today's list is small. However, their hardiness in any situation deserves recognition, and a good choice is provided in the Gardens of the Rose when they flower in early summer.

One of the best, Double White, has small, cupped blooms of fresh fragrance and, when planted with semi-double pink Andrewsii and single purple Mrs Colville, will produce a beautiful hedge. As these roses spread freely by suckering, density is assured, and they may be freely trimmed with shears in winter. A "topiary" bush of one of the marbled pink-and-blush varieties will make a spectacular mound of color in June. Around 1830, hybrids were introduced in America and England: Harison's Yellow and Williams's Yellow, distinguished by stamens or central green eye in bright semi-double flowers.

Scots Briars look well planted on a wild bank with heather and cistus flourish in dry, sandy soil to provide continuous interest. They are among the first roses of summer, poised in delicate, ferny foliage, followed by leaves of autumnal tints and unusual darkest-maroon hips like large blackcurrants.

Stanwell Perpetual

Within a decade of the introduction of this rose in 1839 by Lee of Hammersmith, rose growers were extolling its virtues. An assessment by Thomas Rivers – "one of the sweetest and prettiest of autumnal roses" was repeated by William Prince. The long-flowering period of "large double pale blush flowers of exquisite fragrance" was emphasized by Robert Buist, and, a century on, Edward Bunyard felt it should be in every garden, as this rose was rarely without flowers from May to December.

From its parents, the Autumn Damask and *R. pimpinellifolia*, Stanwell Perpetual gained valuable qualities. It is tolerant of adverse weather conditions, be they drought or frost. Out-growing pliant stems and a naturally lax habit result in a graceful bush requiring space – ideal for a wild area of the garden. However, it may be controlled in a border by attaching the stems to a low perimeter wire firmly pegged to the ground, cutting out old wood and tying down new shoots in August is necessary to keep the whole to 2^1/$_2$ ft, half the normal height. Good gloves are essential for manipulating well-armed stems.

Any account of this rose should include mention of the purple mottling sometimes evident on older foliage. This is innate, not a disease, and does not detract from the overall appeal of this chance seedling from Stanwell – a rose likely to remain popular throughout the world for many years to come.

Portland Rose

This rose looks somewhat similar to *R. gallica* from which it may have been descended. Distinction lies in deeper color and, importantly, a longer flowering habit inherited from the Autumn Damask, Scarlet Four Seasons. It was known in Italy before the end of the eighteenth century and obtained by the Duchess of Portland, an enthusiastic, knowledgeable gardener who exchanged roses with the French Empress Josephine at a time when general trading between the two countries was suspended by war, and it is believed that the French royal gardener, Dupont, named this one for her.

In turn, the Portland Rose gave rise to the development of Rose du Roi, to be known in England as Lee's Perpetual Crimson. With very fragrant, large, semi-double flowers, it has compact form, and the Rose du Roi à Fleur Pourpre varies only in deeper shadings. Robert Buist saw Rose du Roi in England in 1831 and noted that it was carefully fenced in to keep admirers at a distance. Thomas Rivers believed every garden should grow Crimson Perpetual roses for bouquets in August, September, and October on account of beautiful fragrance, rich color and perfect form.

These roses could be used as a low garden hedge of 3 ft, or in limited space where a splash of crimson is needed. With all Portlands it is imperative to carefully deadhead immediately after flowering, allowing each short-stemmed bud to develop fully and flower over a long season.

Comte de Chambord

Of the first Portlands, Rose du Roi played an important part in the development of Hybrid Perpetuals, and a few later fully-double hybrids were originally classed as such and were included by English and American growers in their long lists of that class. But, as these clearly show Damask characteristics, they are now recognized as Portlands.

Comte de Chambord provides an old-rose form in autumn, and, towards the end of October, its full-petalled lilac-pink flowers deepening towards the center are outstanding in the large walled rose garden at Castle Howard. Jacques Cartier has a flatter form of the same color though its small petals are slightly curled. There is a charming white variety, Blanc de Vibert, with a hint of lemon, though this rose is more readily available abroad than in England. Of the darker shades, Arthur de Sansal has small quartered flowers shaded maroon and purple. In Delambre dark pink merges to crimson, and while Marbrée is prettily marbled pale crimson and pink, it has, unlike the others, little scent.

These roses will grace any mixed planting. Over a long period their compact display can prove very useful for central border planting with companions of delicate foliage, like gypsophila, artemesia or polemonium. All Portlands, flowering late, need to be carefully thinned of old wood and reshaped in the spring.

Old Blush China

At the turn of the eighteenth century, a revolution in the world of roses was caused by the introduction to the West of four garden varieties from China. When crossed with old summer flowerers, exciting roses with new characteristics of flower, foliage, color, and important long-flowering habit resulted. One of these, named Parsons's Pink China for its grower at Rickmansworth and probably the same as the Old Blush we grow today, proved a prolific parent.

John Champneys of South Carolina used it with the old white musk (*R. moschata*) to produce Champneys' Pink Cluster, a repeat-flowering climber. From this, Philippe Noisette of Charleston raised Old Blush Noisette, and sent it to his brother Louis in Paris, who established the new class. On the Isle de Bourbon in the Indian Ocean (now Réunion) it was used for hedging with Autumn Damask, a chance cross resulting in the locally named Rose Edouard and subsequent development of Bourbon roses in France.

Old Blush also produced compact China hybrids such as Irene Watts, flat, double, pale pink, and Hermosa, globular, and of deeper shade. The latter was a favorite of George V – he planted thousands at Sandringham in Norfolk. A group of three will make a good show in the average garden, flowering almost incessantly for five months, as does Old Blush itself – an excellent garden rose of 4 x 2 ft which will attain twice that height on a wall.

Cramoisi Supérieur

As important as Old Blush China in rose history, the China rose named *R. semperflorens*, and Slater's Crimson *Rosa*, contributed a new, deep scarlet-crimson and red-tinged foliage to its hybrids and is believed to be responsible for practically all our bright-red long-flowering roses. Unlike Old Blush, its spindly, twiggy growth did not commend it for the garden and it was lost until rediscovered some forty years ago in Bermuda, a regular rose repository for ships trading between East and West.

Of early progeny, Cramoisi Supérieur (1832) received immediate and deservedly long-lasting acclaim for its compact shape of 3 x 2 ft. It bears small double blooms of deepest crimson, typical small, dark, shiny leaves and red prickles. Robert Buist exhorted every American collector to procure one. Twenty years later Thomas Rivers believed there to be no rose more beautiful with "flowers so finely formed … tints so rich". Still later in the century, William Paul rated it amongst the best for constancy of bloom in massed planting. The climbing variety of Cramoisi Supérieur is as spectacular, but flowers less.

Fabvier, a slightly shorter hybrid of the same date, has an occasional streak of white on deep scarlet-crimson, semi-double flowers, and Louis Philippe (1834), with some petals edged blush white, is more readily available in America than elsewhere at present. These early China hybrids made ideal planting for the garden of 1830–40, when the fashion was for small clumps of brilliant color.

Rosa chinensis mutabilis

The origin of this single China, not long known in the west, is obscure. The shade of most true China roses darkens with age, as opposed to usual fading; Mutabilis opens dramatically from a pointed flame-orange bud to a loose, pale buff-yellow flower, changing next day to copper pink and on the third to crimson before dropping. A bush in full flush of every stage is a wonderful sight, worthy of a place in every garden and, moreover, it is hardy and disease-free, flowering from May until the first frosts. Purplish stems bear small, pointed leaves of metallic red tints to complement the flowers perfectly on an open bush of up to 8 ft. It will reach twice that height on a wall, as it does at Kiftsgate Court, in Gloucestershire.

A similar, soft buff-yellow was acclaimed in 1824 with the introduction of Parks's Yellow Tea-Scented China to complete the important quartet, following that of Hume's Blush Tea-Scented China in 1809; both were taken to Prince and Buist in 1828. They had evolved from *R. chinensis* x *R. gigantea*, the Wild Tea Rose, to bestow soft pinks and yellows on subsequent Teas and Hybrid Teas – tenderness of Hume's Blush and Parks's Yellow restricts availability today. They have the same form. They open from oval buds to globular flowers which incline gracefully from a thin, red flower stalk and, within 24 hours on a hot summer day, unfold to loose, double blooms of softly-curving large petals amongst young foliage, burnished red.

Désprez à Fleur Jaune

The influence of Parks's Yellow soon became apparent in some early Noisettes, of which Désprez à Fleur Jaune (1835) is one of the most beautiful of this exceptionally fragrant, long-flowering class of climbers. From a union with Blush Noisette a quartered flower with shades of apricot, yellow, pink, and buff resulted – better planted for close viewing, Buist believed, than at a distance. It was included in the 1848 list of Ashdown Nurseries, Burlington, New Jersey, with thirteen others, some described as "needing slight protection in winter". In England, it reaches 20 x 10 ft on the wall between the first and second collections at Mottisfont.

William Paul, England's leading rosarian of the nineteenth century, regretted the trend to hybridize Noisettes with tender Tea-Scented Roses and of the forty he listed, only eighteen were hardy varieties, useful for any wall situation or as weeping standards and pillars. These included Aimée Vibert, pure white blooms in large clusters, Céline Forestier, shaded yellow-peach of moderate growth, and pale blush Miss Glegg, available in California today.

Tender Lamarque, first of the Tea-Scented Noisettes (1830), has nodding, pale straw-colored flowers and in England must be grown on a very warm, sheltered wall or under glass. An early account from South Carolina told of an 8-year-old example covering a substantial verandah with flowers from May to December. Its seedling, Cloth of Gold thrives beautifully in temperate New Zealand.

Souvenir de la Malmaison

The rose from the Isle de Bourbon reached England via Paris by 1825 and was in America three years later. Subsequent Bourbons charmed William Paul with their clear colors, smooth petals, circular outline, and beautiful foliage. William Buist believed they would become the most widely cultivated roses north of Virginia and, indeed, for a few decades they were in great demand on both sides of the Atlantic.

Souvenir de la Malmaison was collected as an unnamed variety from that garden by the Grand Duke of Russia and, when back in St. Petersburg, he named it to commemorate his visit. The fully quartered, fragrant, creamy-pink flowers recur from June to October, whereas the climbing variety only flowers twice and the early blooms are usually poorly shaped. This last was introduced by Henry Bennett in 1890 and will reach 12 ft in sun or shade. Sixty years later a charming sport of the original was discovered in Ireland, and was named Souvenir de St. Anne's. This variety inherited recurrent flowering with paler flowers of fewer petals making a substantial bush of 7 ft, suitable for the back of a large, mixed border, and accompanied by blue iris for contrast of color and foliage shape.

Coupe d'Hebe and Madame Lauriol de Barny, both soft pink, respond well to and echo the full blooms of their old summer rose ancestors.

Louise Odier

This Bourbon endorses William Paul's admiration of a circular outline and, when lilac-pink Louise Odier first arrived in England from France in 1855, it was advertized as "most distinctive and should be in every collection". Later, Reine Victoria, of the same shape, had deeper pink, almost translucent petals and Madame Pierre Oger brought to the group a creamed blush which deepens in strong sunlight. Planted as a border trio, slender and upstanding, these Bourbons hold their heads high and do not take up a great deal of space. Their form is emphasized by planting softly rotund companions: artemisia, caryopteris and senecio, with neat *Nepeta nervosa* below.

Other Bourbons suit different situations. Commandant Beaurepaire needs space and no distraction to display its dramatic flowers, which appear mainly at midsummer. The 5 x 5 ft bush can be grown alone in grass, where long stems incline gracefully to present cupped blooms splashed with many shades of pink, crimson, and purple. Honorine de Brabant, more delicately striped with purplish tones on pale lilac, grows to 8 ft and two could be used for an archway, or where a moderate climber is needed, although it is not listed as such. The same applies to Madame Isaac Periere, whose voluptuous cerise-magenta blooms have outstanding fragrance and, if grown on the house near a west window, will pervade the room on a summer evening.

Général Jacqueminot

Bourbons remained predominant until about 1850 when they were overtaken by roses arising from an amalgamation of Portlands and Bourbons, known as Hybrid Perpetuals, although they were not perpetual, but *remontant* – flowering well in the autumn. They were acclaimed world-wide until almost the end of the century for their hardiness and large spectacular flowers, excelling at fiercely competitive rose shows. Having so many forebears, the blooms of these roses differ widely: cupped, flat, high-centered, quartered, or rosette and colors range from white to deepest crimson, maroon, and purple, with no yellow among them. Their foliage is rather coarse and bushes, upright or lax, sometimes best displayed with a little manipulation.

Among the earliest varieties, deep-crimson Général Jacqueminot (1853) proved a universal favorite, acclaimed by nurserymen in Europe, America and the Antipodes. Henderson of New York rated it the most fashionable of all roses or winter flowers. The popularly-known "General Jack" produced Charles Lefèbvre, an upright 4 x 3 ft rose with larger crimson-maroon flowers, excellent for exhibiting. A lanky semi-double from the latter, Souvenir du Dr. Jamain, is best planted on a west wall, its even darker purplish-crimson flowers burning in full sun. Tall, blue campanulas make good companions for these dusky roses, with pale violas for underplanting.

Baron Girod de l'Ain

Although shaded, rich reds are often considered the best Hybrid Perpetuals, there are rewarding alternatives. Fragrant flowers of Baron Girod de l'Ain are arresting, with their deckled white edges on cupped petals, the outer leaves reflexing gracefully. A more gentle variety is found in Vick's Caprice, an American introduction of 1897, which has red buds opening to a soft pink, striped blush, on a compact bush. Of clear pink varieties, both Mrs John Laing and Baroness Rothschild grow upright. They have a good scent, the former being particularly useful for cutting. White – rare in this class now – is well represented by the robust Gloire Lyonnaise, which is mentioned in the *Proceedings* of the Pennsylvania Horticultural Society of 1905 as being particularly suitable for Philadelphia's climate. An east-facing position in my own garden provides no deterrent to this pristine example.

Early Hybrid Perpetuals were often disciplined on pillars or by pegging down to form low arches of bloom. This method is also well demonstrated at Mottisfont where 5 ft stems are attached to the base of other bushes. For fronting a border, stout metal tent-pegs provide firm anchorage for the festoons of rich scarlet-crimson Hugh Dickson and the lighter Ulrich Brunner, both of which respond well to this treatment. It is essential with this technique to cut out old stems from the base and train down brittle shoots gradually to avoid snapping.

Général Schablikine

Concurrently with the Hybrid Perpetuals, another class was being developed from the two Tea-Scented Chinas (see p. 36) many of which had new, soft shades of yellow, peach, pink and copper. These less robust tea roses were first kept in conservatories for protection, although some are hardy, for example, brick-red Monsieur Tillier which is excellent for cutting and Général Schablikine, whose coppery-pink blooms are continuously produced, as can be seen near the entrance to the Mottisfont Rose Garden.

However, those that can be grown in Britain in no way compare with the large bushes I have seen flourishing in California and New Zealand, where buff-yellow Safrano, Perle des Jardins, and Solfaterre bloom practically the whole year round. In colder climates, it is worthwhile planting these varieties in suitably large containers for summer enjoyment near the house and transferring to a cool greenhouse or other protection. Buist, for example, advised planting in a perforated barrel to protect against the Pennsylvanian winter.

Whether planted on pots or open ground, Teas should not be pruned until late spring on account of possible damage to soft wood. In extreme winter conditions they may be protected with a covering of small evergreen branches. Alliums, which also appreciate the warmest spot in the garden, prove unobtrusive companions for Tea Roses of subtle shades.

Gloire de Dijon

One of the best-loved climbers since its introduction in 1853, Gloire de Dijon resulted from a cross between a Tea Rose and Souvenir de la Malmaison. It was rated highly for symmetry, size, endurance, color and perfume of flower, and dubbed a "good all-rounder" for every garden purpose by Dean Reynolds Hole, an eminent Victorian rosarian. By 1858 it was advertized in Australia as "the finest tea rose in cultivation" and offered at more than double the price of all other roses by a Melbourne nursery. In England it became popularly known as Old Glory and was said to adorn practically every porch in the Isle of Wight.

The first-recognized Tea Rose, Adam (1825), of like color although more tender, is not listed as a climber but will reach some 8 ft on a sheltered wall. The same situation suits Devoniensis, bred in England (1836) and Sombreuil, both true climbing Teas of moderate height and with pale apricot-tinted centers inside their full white blooms. A century ago, the former was listed among the most satisfactory Teas in California, its climate ideal for this class, whereas Hybrid Perpetuals preferred the rigorous eastern United States. Climbing Lady Hillingdon displays soft apricot flowers with a delicious fragrance over an archway at Wisley Gardens. The delicate refinement of Teas is worthy of protection in rose gardens of today.

Perle d'Or

In 1875 a *R. multiflora* hybrid heralded a new class of small polyantha roses, some showing a marked Tea influence, for example, an orange-cream Perle d'Or. Because of its perfectly-scrolled buds and miniature flowers, it was also known as the buttonhole rose and it makes a slender 4 ft bush. A group of three, backed by delphiniums, is admirable for a yellow-and-blue border planting. Cécile Brunner is half this height, its pale silvery-pink flowers of the same form earning it another name, the Sweetheart Rose, and it looks well when potted for continuous patio display. These charming little roses were immediately appreciated by florists on both sides of the Atlantic.

Confusion sometimes arises between Cécile Brunner and the so-called Bloomfield Abundance (also known as Spray Cécile Brunner), but the distinction lies in the latter's longer calyx lobes. It is also much taller, reaching up to 6 ft, with red stems of open growth and forming a delicate ornamental shrub rose. The climbing form of Cécile Brunner flowers in summer only, but will make a decorative display of up to 25 ft.

In the early part of this century dwarf polyanthas were developed in quantity, and these produced surprising color breaks – the orange-scarlet Gloria Mundi, for example – only to be made redundant by their universally-popular offspring, the floribunda or cluster roses, although they are now making a comeback.

Rosa rugosa alba

At the end of the eighteenth century *rugosas* were brought to Europe from the Far East, where they had long been cultivated and used domestically. Another century elapsed, however, before they reached our gardens. This species has large flowers blooming over many months with dark-green glossy foliage turning gold, orange-red hips high in vitamin C content and very prickly stems, often put to good use as an impenetrable hedge. White *R. r. alba* is more desirable than *R. r. typica*, as the latter's vivid pink blooms clash with fruit. They are disease resistant and will tolerate poor soil and harsh weather, thereby proving ideal roadside planting and controlling sand erosion, naturalizing on eastern American coasts.

When thoughts turned to wild gardens under the influence of William Robinson in 1883, breeders capitalized on obvious *rugosa* qualities and the list is long today. A selection of four for the average garden might include rich-crimson-purple Roseraie de l'Hay, soft yellow Agnes (both substantial bushes of up to 6 ft), slightly-smaller creamy-white Schneezwerg, which has orange-red hips, and, of a more compact form, Fru Dagmar Hastrup, whose pale-pink blooms associate well with crimson hips. They need no support and will provide lasting interest in the garden with their bold, fragrant flowers, lively foliage, and conspicuous fruit.

Alberic Barbier

A change of rose fashion occurred at the end of the nineteenth century, Alberic Barbier being among the first of new, small-flowered, pliant-stemmed ramblers. These were a welcome contrast to large formal blooms which dominated the previous era and were eminently suitable for decorative gardening. With hybridization between two vigorous fragrant species from the Far East and new roses of varied color, a wonderful medley was produced.

Alberic Barbier inherited typical glossy *R. wichuraiana* foliage, its soft, yellow-cream loose flowers from tea rose Shirley Hibberd continuing well into the autumn. This has always been a favorite, as has the coppery-ink Albertine which came later from the same French breeder. Both inherited lengthy growth, reaching 20 ft. In contrast, *R. multiflora* makes a dense spreading bush of 12 ft, with large trusses of tiny, single white flowers. The yellow-cream hybrid Goldfinch will also make an excellent bushy shrub.

Ramblers should have old wood cut out after flowering and new growth should be carefully trained in position for the next year's display. Some Wichuraianas can be allowed to ramble on the ground. This trailing species was originally known in America as the Memorial Rose on account of its wide use in cemeteries. Multifloras tend to flower early so a careful choice will spread the once-flowering ramblers over a maximum period.

Rosa moyesii

Wild roses are indigenous only in the Northern Hemisphere, and of the known 140 species, *R. moyesii* is outstanding and probably the most spectacular in terms of flower and fruit. It was discovered by E. H. Wilson in Western Hupeh, China, when collecting for Kew Gardens and the Arnold Arboretum in Boston, and was named by him for a hospitable missionary, the Rev. J. Moyes. Growth is tall (12 ft), with a slender outline below long branches curving outwards from the top to form an umbrella for shade-loving plants below. The early, deep crimson-red flowers are borne along these high stems from which large flagon-shaped hips dangle in autumn.

China is the most prolific source of beautiful wild roses and some were collected by missionaries; for example, *R. hugonis* by a Father Hugh. This grows to a rounded 7 ft bush with ferny foliage and tiny, single primrose-yellow flowers that always remain cupped. The hips are small and dark and unspectacular, but this species presents a fresh spring picture.

R. omiensis pteracantha from Western China is an unusual rose. It has only four delicate white petals and enormous flat blood-red prickles randomly placed on bristly stems. This 10 ft species should be planted where sunlight from behind will fire them more intensely. They turn dull after the first season, and stems must be cut from the base to encourage spectacular new growth.

Index

chapter 14

My gym bag is on my lap. I am holding on to it with both hands. I wonder if it looks strange, how I'm holding it so tight. Tisha is sitting right next to me.

Now I'm starting to freak. What if they know? All that stuff I wrote. And there's stuff about Tisha, too. Not anything bad, but. What if she gets into trouble because of me? *Well, Kurt, you've done it again. Get the girl you really like in trouble with the principal. That would have to be the loser move of the century.* I try to force the thought out of my head. I try to force it out. Looking around I notice the bull pen is pretty empty. Just me and Tisha and a couple other kids way down at the other end. This big-ass area where students are herded like cattle, put in seats, and told to wait to see one of the VP's or the man himself, Principal Roberts. All the kids call it the bull pen, like in baseball. But if you get sent down here, it's not to pitch. It usually means detention, or worse . . . Didn't used to be all open like this, but they redid it after the murder last year. They said it was more secure like this.

Roberts's secretary looks nervous. She's not looking at anyone. Her head's buried in some papers. All the loud yelling coming from the office is not making me feel any better about being here.

NO WAY! Tisha's smile takes me by surprise; she's staring right at me. She looks like she's going to say something to me. Those beautiful lips, and the way her cheeks rise up so high on her face . . . I loosen my grip on my gym bag. I should just put it on the floor, like a normal person . . . but I can't. I have to have my gym bag close. I might have to do something. I am so close. So close to doing something, so close to doing what I think about doing every day . . . What I've thought about doing every day since I stopped being me and became Dirt. I hate Dirt. I wish Dirt was dead. I want to be me again, like I used to be. Maybe the time has come. Time to take a stand. Get rid of the ones who keep me down. Maybe this is how I can be me again. Start at the top. Why not? I could do it, I could . . .

Even with Tisha next to me, I could do it . . . Just calmly walk into his office, unzip my gym bag, and—

"So what are *you* down here for?" I wasn't expecting to hear her voice. My heart starts beating fast; my face gets flushed. For a minute, I think I was speaking out loud. All my thoughts out in the open for her to hear.

It takes me a few seconds to realize she is speaking to *me*. I instinctively look over my shoulder, expecting someone else to be there, the person she's actually speaking to. BUT no one is there. Just me. She is *speaking* to *me*. All of a sudden I feel embarrassed. I lower my gym bag to the floor and shift in my seat. Say something back; just say anything . . . I turn towards Tisha and smile. My mouth opens, welcoming the words that are about to come out.

The yelling in the office is getting louder . . .

"I don't know. They just called me dow—" The sound of the office door being slammed open stops everything in the bull pen.

Roberts's secretary lets out a scream. Tisha looks horrified. I am just pissed I didn't get a chance to finish my sentence . . . I *never* catch a break.

Tisha

"So what are *you* down here for?" As soon as I say it, I wish I'd said it differently. I hope I didn't sound like I thought he was in trouble or something. I just wanted to say something. Shoot, *I'm* probably in trouble, and I don't even know what I did. I should really thank Kurt for helping me pick up my books that time. He probably doesn't remember anyway. What's he lookin' at? He's so shy . . . Dag, what's goin on in the principal's office? Kurt's got a nice smile; he should smile more. I should tell him that. That would be a good thing to say . . .

"I don't know. They just called me dow—" I feel myself jump back in my chair. I want to run out of here but I can't move. My heart is beating a million miles an hour. That door was so loud. Slamming against the wall, the sound was sickening. Mrs. Tinsley's scream gives me a chill down my back. I wish I could scream. I can't do anything but sit here, frozen like a big block of ice. I feel like I'm going to be sick. Sometimes I throw up when I get scared . . . I really hope I don't throw up.

I wish Tiny was here . . .

Floater

I feel the warmth before I feel the wetness. Now the dark spot forms, but I'm the only one who seems to notice. The fact that I've just pissed myself is the last thing on anyone's mind in this office. I can't catch my breath, and I feel like I'm going to puke. My hand is shaking and sweat is pouring down my face. To look at me, you'd think I was just sprayed with a garden hose.

This is the first time in my life that I'm actually *not* hungry. I haven't eaten since seven this morning, but the thought of food is making me gag. Why the hell didn't I leave earlier? I didn't have to stay, but I *had* to see what happened.

Had to see the fruits of my labor. Fuck me. So full of myself standing there leaning against Roberts's desk, touching it like it was my prize. Both of us congratulating each other on our impending victory. Damn, I should've left when I had the chance. So stupid of me. And now—

"You've got piss running down your leg, son. What kind of weak faggot are you?" I guess someone did notice. The crazed man's voice pushes me back, like an unseen force, pushing me back into Roberts's desk.

I call him the crazed man, but we know who he is, don't we?

Colonel James P. Duncan, decorated war hero, respected member of the community. Complete psycho.

"You make me sick, boy." Colonel Duncan has the blade of the knife pushed against Roberts's Adam's apple. From the look of the few drops of blood collecting under Roberts's chin, I'd say the thing is sharp. Colonel Duncan orders us to stand in front of the office door, our backs to him. This is not good . . . I am trying to pretend this isn't really happening; it can't be. It's too fucked up. This crazed bastard has totally fucked everything up. Everything I've worked for, all those twisted moments, leading up to what should have been my coming-out party. Now he's about to piss it all away. Actually, he's making me piss it all away. If I could do something, I would, but I can't. I am powerless. I can't call anyone, get some thug to do my dirty work for me. No, all I can do is just stand here and piss on myself. Standing at attention. Watching Colonel Duncan get ready to slice up my ticket to paradise.

The sound of the office door slamming against the wall makes my ears ring. I almost fall on my face as I get pushed out into the bull pen.

If I could still pee, there would be a flood on the floor by now.

I glance over at Roberts; he looks like a man who has given up.

He looks like he knows the end is coming soon.

Fuck that. I'm not giving up. I've been through too much to have it end like this.

Too much . . .

Ryan

I'm feeling better. Better with every step I take, on my way to the office. Things are going to be alright. Roberts backed down. I knew he would. I knew I would win; Duncans always win—

I hear the voice before I see the face. I know instantly who it is. Everything I had hoped for just five seconds ago is gone. It's all gone.

I stop short of the bull pen. Staying out of sight.

Kids are starting to come out of classrooms, wondering what all the noise is about. I take a quick peek into the bull pen. The scene that greets me is a complete freak show but I shouldn't be surprised. He finally snapped. The crazy bastard finally snapped. I see the knife just for a few seconds. Shit, that's his combat knife. An original F.S. fighting knife from World War II. Told me he got it at an auction. He called it a killing blade . . .

I am hit with the sudden realization of what I have to do. Everything is clear. *This has to stop.* The words on the tip of my tongue. *This has to stop.* Now they come out, in a whisper. *This has to stop.*

I take two steps forward, his words becoming clear now. I don't hear him.

I don't care what he's saying. It doesn't matter anyway. It's too late for words.

Too late . . .

Floater

"GET THE GODDAMN PAPERS OR I'M GOING TO SLIT HIS THROAT."

Mrs. Tinsley is pretending to rummage through her desk, looking for the imaginary papers that will pardon the Duncan kid.

That psycho told Roberts he was going to give him one chance to fix everything. When a maniac comes into your office and says he's going to give you a chance, you say

Okay. You don't tell him there's nothing you can do. You're supposed to lie *before* the knife is at your throat. Doesn't he ever go to the movies? Now this bogus paper hunt. How long does he think Colonel Crazy is going to go for this? Not very long. Roberts is such a moron.

"WHERE ARE THOSE GODDAMN PAPERS?"

I must look like shit. Piss all over myself, and right in front of Tisha.

I wonder if she read my note yet? I could make a break for it, but I'd never make three feet. That crazy fuck would slice us both up before I even got my fat ass to the hallway. OUCH, fucker's twisting my arm.

He spins me and Roberts around, so we're facing the entrance to the bull pen. He's still behind us, but now he's standing next to Mrs. Tinsley's desk.

She's shuffling papers frantically. There's no way she can keep this up much longer.

Where the hell is security, they should be here by now . . .

T i s h a

"WHERE ARE THOSE GODDAMN PAPERS?"

This seems like a real bad movie playing right in front of me. But I know this is real; this is not a movie. This is really happening. All I can think of is Jake. Dead on the bathroom floor. Pools of blood collecting around his mouth. Every detail of that morning coming back. Coming back so clear it's like it's happening all over again. I'm not gonna end up like him, no way. I can't let this go on. I must be crazy, too, but I can't let this guy do this. I can do something. I know I can. If I don't do something, this guy is going to kill us all. We're *all* gonna end up like Jake.

He's probably got something more than just that knife. He's got that look in his eyes, like he doesn't care. *Now* he's got Principal Roberts and that Mark kid—facing the *other* way. The crazy man's back is to me.

Maybe I can sneak up on him. Maybe . . .

"Kurt, I'm going to do something. I have to stop this." I stand up, almost instinctively.

"Tisha, don't." Kurt looks scared. He looks like he can't believe I'm standing. I can't either. Kurt shakes his head, staring at me like I'm out of my mind. Maybe I am but I have to go through with this.

"Tisha, are you crazy? Don't, he'll kill you. Just wait, wait . . . I have a plan."

"Really?" I whisper back. I think he'd tell me anything at this point.

Kurt is begging me to sit down. If he could scream it, I'm sure he would. The guy is getting angrier. He's getting even louder, pushing that Mark kid around. I can't stop thinking about how his uniform has no wrinkles. Its perfect, everything in place. Every medal shining on his lapel. He looks so professional, he looks so together . . . Why is he acting so crazy? . . . My bravery tries to slip away. I won't let it, but reality is sinking in.

How do you stop a crazy man?
I finally sit down and whisper to Kurt, "What are you
gonna do?"
He doesn't say anything.
I hope it's a good plan.
A real good plan . . .

chapter 15

"WHERE ARE THOSE GODDAMN PAPERS?"

His voice is gravelly, like a smoker who has screamed his
whole life.

His eyes are what I see first, darting wildly in all direc-
tions. Then I see the knife. It looks like one of those
knives from an old war movie.

Long skinny blade . . . Looks sharp as hell.

The blade is making little flashes of light from the high-
beam fluorescents hitting it from above.

Damn, that dude looks mean. Roberts looks like he's afraid
he's gonna die. He's got that look like he's already dead.

The kid's got a big wet spot on his pants. Serves him right. I
hate that kid; he's that snitch, always thinks he's better than
everyone else, too. The guy looks like he's a military officer
or something. He's got ribbons and stuff on his jacket, and
he's got one of those cool beret hats I saw on that *Killer
Combat* show. The soldier guy's got the knife under
Roberts's chin and he keeps pushin' the kid and pullin' his
arm back. He turns them around. Damn, he must be strong.
He barely notices me and Tisha, sitting behind him. He
just keeps screaming at the secretary about some papers.
This dude is whacked.

He looks crazy, but kinda cool at the same time.

"Kurt, I'm going to do something. I have to stop this."

"Tisha, don't." Tisha is halfway out of her chair before
I can get the words out of my mouth.

"Tisha, are you crazy? Don't, he'll kill you. Just wait,
wait . . . I have a plan."

"Really?" She sounds like she doesn't believe me.

"Yeah, but you have to sit down. Come on, sit back down." Now I'm pleading with her. Slowly she sits back down. Fortunately, the soldier guy is too busy yelling to notice what's going on.

I have a plan. Yeah, right. I had to say something. She was gonna get herself killed. What was she gonna do anyway? Man, that girl is brave.

"What are you gonna do?" Tisha whispers. I don't answer.

My gym bag is under my chair. I push it very slowly with both feet, bringing it forward. I can tell Tisha is watching what I'm doing.

Why should I risk my life for Roberts and his little snitch? What did they ever do for me? I *know* they wouldn't save my ass if the situation was reversed.

But Tisha, she was going to actually try to stop that crazy dude. She is so amazing.

What the *hell* am I gonna do?

R y a n

"I WANT THOSE GODDAMN PAPERS AND I WANT THEM RIGHT NOW.

"WHERE THE HELL IS MY SON! YOU BETTER GET ME MY SON! DO NOT UNDERESTIMATE MY RESOLVE."

He's screaming like a maniac. He's really lost it now. He sounds crazier than I've ever heard him. He's so full of shit. He doesn't give a crap about me. This is just fun for him. Sick fun.

Well, I'm about to rain on his twisted parade . . . two more steps and I'm in. Two more steps . . .

"I'm right here, sir. Drop the knife and let them go. Do not underestimate *my* resolve."

Floater

Shoot the crazy bastard. I said that in my head. I wanted to say it out loud, but the way things are going for me, the gun's probably not even loaded.

Ryan looks too calm, too in control. I don't like that. I think he's going to do it. I think he's really gonna off his old man. He looks like he could shoot us all.

I really hope that thing isn't loaded. Looks like a Glock— how did he get that thing into school anyway? Past the metal detectors? They never check the jocks.

Fuck, does it even matter now?

I should've left when I had the chance . . . Now every-thing is fucked. I can't get my money from the geek squad, my great plan evaporating right before my eyes. And . . .

my lovely Tisha . . .
oh, Tisha . . .

"Where did you get that, son?"

"You gave it to me, remember? My 'just in case'?"

"I don't know what you're talking about, but I'm giving you about five seconds to give me that gun or you're going to be really sorry."

"Sorry? Sorry for what? Sorry that you're my father? Sorry that you regularly beat the shit out of me for no reason? Sorry because you don't even care about *me*, really? All you care about is Ryan Duncan, the all-American football player. The only reason you're here is because of *you*, not me. You just want the glory; you just want to be able to say that I'm your kid, be able to tell all your buddies how you made me, how it was all because of you . . . Well, you can tell *this* to your buddies. I fucked up. That's right, Mr. Roberts. Kim told the truth. I did what they said I did. I'm really a fuckup, Dad. I can't control myself. I have a problem—I have problems. How do you like that, huh? Your perfect son is really a fuckup. What do you think of that?"

"You don't know what you're saying. They've got you all turned around. It's this damn school, all these faggots runnin' around . . ."

"It's not the school; it's me. It's me. You know why I'm the way I am? Because I learned everything I know from

you. You're *so* warped. Look at you; you're a disgrace.
A disgrace to yourself, to your family, to your country.
What would Mom think if she was here? You're a dis-
grace to her memory—"

"You'd better watch that mouth, son. Now drop your
weapon or I will put you in a world of hurt. Drop your
weapon. That is a direct order."

"I already *am* in a world of hurt. What the hell can you
do to me now? No matter what I did . . . captain of the
football team, an all-American . . . you never said shit—
not one thing that ever made me think you loved me,
even a little bit—nothin'. Nothin' but your belt. Well,
fuck it. I'm sick of all this shit, and it's all gonna stop
right now. So I'm going to tell you one last time, put
down the knife and let them go.
   "*That* is a direct order. Do not underestimate *my*
resolve."

Dark and quiet

I don't even remember getting up. It was all in super-
super slow motion. Tisha turning to me, nodding her
head, like she knew what I was going to do before I did.
Me, looking at this totally bizarre scene playing itself out.
Knowing that this was not going to have a happy ending.
Realizing that soldier boy is standing with his back to me.
Completely oblivious to the fact that I am sitting right
behind him.

The captain of the football team, screaming and pointing that gun into his father's face. I don't think he'd notice if the roof fell in.

I don't remember getting up. But before I know it, I am UP. On my feet *swinging* my gym bag at the back of the crazy man's head. *Swinging* like I had a Louisville slugger and it was the bottom of the ninth. *Swinging* with all of my hate, and anger, and fear, *swinging* at the heads of everyone who ever cut me—put me—DOWN—turned me into Dirt, turned me into Dirt . . . *Swinging* . . . I watch the crazy man stagger to his left, falling—fast over the desk, the knife flying out of his hands, landing safely away. He just misses the secretary as he crashes to the floor. Roberts races out of the bull pen, the snitch who peed himself right behind. I see Tisha out of the corner of my eye, standing up, moving towards me . . .

I hear screams and yelling and running getting closer—sounding like an army approaching.

Sprinting into the bull pen, they tackle the quarterback first. Then they jump on top of that crazy man. I don't move, I can't.

I feel the weight of someone big on my back. Before I know it, I am at the bottom of a big pile. Bodies on top of me grabbing and punching . . .

I can't breathe. I can't breathe . . .

Then
everything stops.
No motion, no sound.
Nothing.
Everything is dark.

Everything is
dark
and
quiet.

chapter 16

Floater's walk . . .

This is Mandy Montgomery, reporting live from Rockville High School, where on the one-year anniversary of the murder of Jake Stiles, yet another tragedy was just barely averted. Details are still sketchy but what we do know is that a crazed parent took the principal and a student hostage . . .

In a bizarre twist, the crazed parent was apparently confronted by his son, who had a gun . . . I will have more on this developing story throughout the afternoon . . .

I'm walking . . . Walking past everything and everyone . . . Cameras and reporters, cops, firemen . . .

Mandy Montgomery looks like a little kid on Christmas day. She must live for this stuff. I smell like piss and sweat, and I've never been so hungry in my life.

But I don't stop, not for Mandy, not for the cops, not even for Tisha.

I'm just going to keep walking, keep walking all the way home . . .

Then I'm going to eat everything in the house . . .

Tisha in the car . . .

Mom is so scared, I can see her hands shaking on the steering wheel . . . She hasn't stopped hugging me since I got in the car . . . That Mark kid looks like he just came back from a war or something . . . The police said we

could go home, for now. I didn't see what happened to
Kurt. They were on top of him so fast, then it was just a
blur . . . Everything happening all at once . . . I hope he
doesn't get in trouble.

They took Principal Roberts away in an ambulance . . .
they said just for observation..
Mom is crying now . . . She's got Dad on the cell phone . . .
I'm sooooo tired . . .
I'm just glad I'm alive . . .

Tiny is going to trip when she hears about this . . .
She is going to *trip* . . .

The wicked witch is dead.

"I had to do it. I didn't have a choice."
"I didn't have a choice . . ." I'm trying to convince the
paramedic who's stitching my eye that I had to pull a gun
on my own father. He is nodding his head, like you might
do to a crazy person. My back is itching, but I can't
scratch it because of the handcuffs . . . The paramedic is
talking to me now, speaking slowly like I was a child.
Like I really *was* crazy . . .
But, I know I'm not crazy. I've never felt saner in my life.
Fuckin' security smashed up my eye really good.
I didn't even see them coming.
All I saw was that kid whackin' the Colonel in the back
of the head with his gym bag . . . What was in that thing?
Man, that took balls . . . That kid, I don't even know his
name . . . The dude must have ice water in his veins . . .

They say I might get charged, but I don't care . . . I'm free . . . The wicked witch is dead.

The twisted Colonel is going to jail . . . That's good enough for me . . . I hope he rots . . .

A Hero is born

Mandy: This is Mandy Montgomery reporting live from Rockville High School, where new details are emerging from this afternoon's near tragedy . . .

Everyone is looking at me, but it's different now . . . They think I saved them . . . They're saying things, pointing and staring at me . . . But in a different way . . . Where's Tisha? I really want to talk to her . . . If it wasn't for her— I hope this doesn't take too long—Wow, Mandy is even hotter up close . . .

Mandy: The hero student's name is Kurt Reynolds, and we are lucky enough to have him right here. Kurt, can you tell us in your own words what happened? I understand you were the one who actually knocked the knife out of Colonel Duncan's hands. How did you do it? How does it feel to be a hero? Your parents must be so proud. Is there anything you want to say to them? Do you have anything to say to the youth of America?

The bright lights are blinding. It hurts to open my eyes all the way . . . Told me to go talk to Mandy. They said I was going to be on TV . . . I just want to go home . . . Can you believe that? All I want to do is go home, lay my head down, and sleep . . . Just sleep . . .

Mandy: Kurt, we are *live,* you know. Do you have anything to say to them? The youth of America?

Kurt: What do I have to say to the youth of America?

Good luck . . .

coda

It's midnight and I can't sleep. This could very well be my last night on earth. My last night as Floater. The late word is that Roberts is going to get fired. The McConnell girl's charge, the murder last year . . . and with what happened today with that psycho . . . Too many hits to take . . . no one could survive that. Not even crafty Ronny Roberts. There's going to be a housecleaning, top to bottom. Maybe the whole administration.

That notebook thing blew up in my face, too. I got a call from one of my "sources." Can you believe somebody snitched on *me*? What is this world coming to. Some kid claims he saw me take the notebook from Kurt's locker. He said he saw me writing in it. Kid went and told Vice-Principal Shavers. You know Shavers will try to use this to save his own butt. He's on a sinking ship, every man for himself. Oh, well, I guess "hero boy" Kurt will be around a little longer.

Hey, I tried. Don't blame me when that time bomb goes off. Doesn't matter, I won't be around for the fallout.

Tomorrow morning a new day will dawn. An entirely different reality, a different universe where I no longer exist. Well, to be perfectly honest, a place where I couldn't exist. Even if Roberts stayed, how could I? How could I go back to just being Mark Daniels, junior at Rockville High? Just another nameless fat-faced loser with the added tag of the kid who pissed himself when the going got a little tough. No, not me, not after everything I've been through . . . Tomorrow morning is something I've dreaded for a long time, but it's not something I haven't planned for. One thing you should remember is that I'm always a step ahead. Oh yeah, I've made my calls, given my mom the old sob story. "I don't feel safe anymore at Rockville. I am emotionally scarred by the day's events." She bought it.

If things go the way I hope they do, in a week I will be enrolled at Norwood. How does the saying go? The enemy of my enemy is my friend? Our arch rivals and future state champs . . .

Hey, free enterprise, and I go to the highest bidder. From what I understand, they are in need of someone with some very specific skills. Someone who can get them what they need, someone who can keep the peace . . . I heard they need a new pair of ears, a new set of eyes, their man on the inside . . . Someone like . . . Floater. There will be sacrifices to make, Tisha for one, but . . . I suppose: "Just knowing she is in the world will have to be enough . . ." At least for now.

Now

I have to keep my eye on the prize . . . With Roberts getting all the heat, I get off scot-free. I've got no shit on my shoes, just a little piss in my pants . . . I am still the man with the golden tongue, Johnny-on-the-spot.

The ultimate weapon—the new twenty-first-century spy. Don't cry for me. I'll be alright.

You know why?

Because, I'm a genius

and I'm beyond you . . .

remember . . .

It's gonna be OK

I'm gonna make everything right, with Susie . . . with Kim . . . I'm gonna get help . . . I need help; I know that now . . . It's been too much, all these years . . . fighting this war . . . It's just been too much . . . But now it's over. The war is finally over. I'll get Susie back; I'll play again . . .
I know I will.
It's gonna be OK. I really think it's gonna be OK . . .

"LIGHTS OUT."

Beginning

I'm upstairs in my secret lair. Been watching Kurt all night, on all the stations. He mentioned my name every time. He said I was the one who gave him the courage to stop Colonel Duncan. That was real cool, but I don't know if it's true. Tiny called, to make sure I was alright. I didn't feel like going out tonight. Tiny said she was too upset to eat. Too worried about me.
I talked to Kurt a little while ago. It was real nice to talk to him. Real nice . . .
I'm so tired. I can't even think straight.
Mom and Dad said I was brave. They said they love me so much.
They said a lot through their tears . . .
I haven't even cried yet. Is that weird?
Somethin's changed, though . . .

I feel different now.
Somethin' changed *me* in the bull pen today.
I don't feel as afraid; I don't feel as lost. I don't feel like
I'll melt away in the sun.

I'm beginning to know who I am now.

I'm beginning to know

who I am . . .

Hope

I am home. Under the covers. Lights are out.
I was interviewed by six different news stations tonight.
Mandy Montgomery gave me an autographed picture of
herself. It's up on my wall, next to my poster of Misty
Manic riding a Harley.

My parents are treating me different now, like I'm a
star, like I did something really important. That was a
quick change. Maybe I'll give them the benefit of the
doubt. At least for now.

It was so great to talk to Tisha tonight. Maybe I *will* get
the girl, like in the movies. Maybe I will . . .

I'm so tired, I could sleep for days. I'm supposed to be
on The Morning Show tomorrow with Tisha. That should
be real cool, if I get up in time.

My gym bag is under my bed now; no one even looked
inside.

Man, they would have been surprised . . .

Mr. Tanner called me. He said that I was a hero. I told him I didn't know what that meant. I told him I just did what I did. What I had to do.
He said that he was proud of me and that I was a very special person.
Special, no one's ever called me that before . . . I like that . . . I like being special . . .

I feel good, like I used to when I was younger. I feel like it's the past, only it's the present. Does that make any sense? I want to keep this feeling. I want to always feel like this, like I'm OK and things are going to be OK and I'm not going to have to eat shit every day and my parents will understand me more, and . . . not ignore me and . . . everything will be like it was . . .
Like it is now.
I hope this feeling lasts forever . . .

I hope . . .